MW00623893

"Nothing wasted, no extra constructs *The Memory House*. Every sentence a small satisfaction to read; some lines punch and others pull readers into the dust and sweetness of what is remembered/misremembered/passed down. Part document, part multi-generational memoir, and one hundred and fifty percent relevant, *The Memory House* shows us family, war, borders, home, persecution, necessity, longing, belonging, and migration as infinite loops. From the Middle East to the Midwest, from the early 1900's to now, Raki gives us entry into the stories she carries in her marrow - an heirloom she offers up in words to us."

-**Franciszka Voeltz**, author of
All this Blue, All this Broken

"In this slight memoir, trauma and struggle—war, immigration, refugee crises, imprisonment, hunger—claw their way from past decades into today's tragedies. But housed within that harsh narrative, the tenderness of day-to-day life delicately webs between generations, passed from saba and safta to mother to child. This is the history woven within Jewish families, and looped between endlessly, in a square of chocolate, in tomato and cucumber salad, in fields of sunflowers and orchards full of oranges, in one-room buildings full of beds and uncertain ships crossing the sea. The organic, elusive structure of *The Memory House* hints at how our family's stories, both shared and withheld, nurture unnamed hungers and connections within us all."

-**Miriam McNamara**, author of
The Unbinding of Mary Reade

"Raki Kopernik offers a work of autobiography that transcends the self and honors the cultural webs her family wove long before her, their struggles to make a good life, suffering displacement and adapting to create a home. This work is spare and lyrical, minutely observed and emotionally resonant. *The Memory House* addresses themes of time, place, family, and memory to explore issues of dislocation and concepts of home. The result is a book full of power, subtlety, and beauty."

-**Ryan Berg**, author of
No House to Call My Home: Love, Family, and Other Transgressions

The Memory House

Raki Kopernik

First Edition

Printed by amazon-kindle

Paperback ISBN: 978-0-578-49061-8

Cover Design by Allison Ward
Interior design, typesetting, and illustrations by Brian Fox, Adrian A. Gonzalez, Alonna L. Heller, Alexandra Meidl, & Claire Schultz

Muriel Press
Marian University Wisconsin
45 S. National Ave,
Fond du Lac, WI 54935

murielpress@marianuniversity.edu

MURIEL PRESS

For the Drorim

Table of Contents

We are not made of angles.

There is no one way, no one straight line, no one yes no. All of our stories, different loops, same spirals. Same different same. We are made of woven circles.

Adam from the Hebrew = man/person

Adama from the Hebrew = earth

We are one species.

There was a time when there were no gardens. The land was beige and dusty, the water sparse. The only fruit the prickly pear, difficult to harvest through long spikes. Even those cacti were brought over from Mexico.

Back then, before they lived there and for a short while after, the British owned the land. A small piece the size of New Jersey in the middle of the middle of the Middle East.

A tender heart at the barely visible center.

There is so much space like it for thousands of miles around, but everyone wants the sweet middle. The core. What they think is the soul.

Borders are imaginary lines made up by people.

1.

My mother lived on a moshav. There were no real houses when they arrived. Everything was dust, like the beginning of time. The color beige and the smell of earth baking in the hot sun. They lived in a one-room apartment in an old British airport hanger divided into pieces, a long loaf of bread sliced into thick chunks. Each family had a slice, side-by-side. There were no windows. No plumbing, no electricity, a shared outhouse. The floors were desert sand and they hauled water from a reservoir in metal buckets.

My mother saw her brother being born on that dirt floor.

I asked my mother about her first memory.

She remembers a dog barking behind a screened door, its mouth full of sharp teeth and drool, its legs taller than her three-year-old self.

She remembers being scared.

Her memory could have been any year, any country. When she was three, the world could not have imagined itself into what it was when I was three.

On her fourth birthday, a girl stole my mother's apple juice.

There was only one cup of juice per person.

There was one small piece of sweet cake made with eggs,
sugar, flour, and margarine, no butter. Butter was as rare as
chocolate. Chocolate was as rare as an indoor toilet.

There was one white dress she got to wear on that birthday
with one red anemone flower stitched on it, and a string that
hung around her neck with a faded blue paper *4* attached.
Made by her teenage teacher.

And a birthday wreath of wildflower weeds to wear on her head.

These stories my mother told me, the memories they invoked from my own childhood. As though I were my mother's sister, my Safta's daughter.

Our memories tangle into a single memory house.

My mother and her brother played with small stones dug up from the dusty ground in front of their house, stacked the stones high until they tumbled.

Once, they ran through the tall wheat fields that surrounded the moshav. My mother thought the wheat would feel soft on her skin, like fine baby hair. She liked the *shhh* sound it made when the wind blew.

The wheat didn't feel the way it looked. It was scratchy. And much taller than she thought. She half closed her eyes as she ran.

There is a residue in wheat that rubs off when disturbed, stains skin a deep black.

My mother and her brother laughed at each other. Her brother's eyes whiter against the residue, though his skin wasn't much lighter. He was darker than the rest of the family. That's how they knew there was Sephardic in their blood.

The moshav was in Afula, in the north. My mother and her parents moved there in 1948 from the kibbutz where she was born. War broke for declaration of the state of Israel. The kibbutz was on the border of Gaza, women and children evicted, men stayed to fight.

It was a short war and when it was over, Israel was still Israel. But no one knew when it would suddenly not be Israel.

The British gave residents trees to plant, orange and grapefruit, and ducks and chickens. There were always, and sometimes only eggs to eat.

Safta, my grandmother, fed the chicks hard-boiled eggs, grated and scattered on the ground. My mother was too little to think it strange for baby chickens to eat their hard- boiled siblings. She watched chicks waddle, tiny and soft, pecking at their food like nothing mattered.

Each family got a field of something to grow for trade and income, wheat, watermelon, sunflowers.

I remember the sunflower fields, enormous bright yellow heads like a thousand suns all the way to the border, too many to count, a blanket I could wrap my eyes in. Their seeds stuck in my teeth.

They lived in the bread loaf airport hanger until her brother was three and she was six. When the two room houses were built, every family got one of those, too.

My mother was born in the kitchenette of a one-room house on the kibbutz.

Her brother was born on the dirt floor of the airport hanger.

Their baby brother was born in the hospital.

When Safta went into labor, my mother and her brother were left with older friends who also spoke Hungarian and had endured the Holocaust. They lost their families, and so became tied to ours.

In the years after World War II, it was common to make new family with survivors.

The family friends' house smelled like eggs and cabbage. They fed my mother noodli, a potato noodle dish sprinkled with sugar and cinnamon.

The wife looked like a safta, her hands stained with liver spots, her bosom hulking under a floral print dress that hung around her body like a tablecloth.

The wife asked my mother if she wanted to be her child, if she wanted to go on tractor rides, said she would buy my mother a raincoat.

She once had a daughter who died after two days. After that, she was no longer able to have children.

Saba, my grandfather, left Romania first in 1940, as Europe became heated with anti- Semitism. People banded together on illegal boats to find freedom in British ruled Palestine.

Some people made it.

Some were sent back to Europe.

Some were sent to prison camps in Cypress.

Some drowned.

Saba's boat made it safely to Palestine and he became free. He sent word to Safta to join him. She was afraid, but could no longer work in Europe, could no longer walk alone down the street, buy groceries at the market, talk to anyone in public. If she stayed she would be killed for being Jewish like many of her friends.

If she boarded an illegal boat, she could drown.

She could die in a camp.

Or, she could make it.

This picture of Safta through my mother's words and the wrinkled photographs in Safta's attic, a resilient imprint when I close my eyes and listen.

Holocaust museums every year, I always knew what the 1940's looked like.

When we were kids, we called gaunt people *concentration camp victims.*

Upon landing in Palestine, Safta's boat was captured by the British and taken to Atlit. Atlit was a twenty-five acre prison detention camp south of Haifa.

Eastern European refugees tried to escape war, so the British built prison camps to contain them.

My grandparents left anti-Semitic Europe to arrive in anti-Semitic Palestine.

Three quarters of a century later, in 2016, Syrian refugees on illegal boats, same, trying to escape into Europe. Same thing. Same.

Atlit was a prison, surrounded by barbed wire, guarded by British soldiers in watchtowers. Seven pm curfew, men and women separated, one hour visitation for married couples. Babies born inside corrugated metal barracks.

On entrance, prisoners had to strip naked and wait in line for a shower, just like German concentration camps.

Some people came to Atlit from places like Auschwitz. They had forgotten the comfort of real showers.

Atlit was a prison for Jews, not a concentration camp, but a prison. For Jews, not criminals. People who were different, the same, same different.

Like in concentration camps, prisoners didn't know when, if ever, they would be released.

My mother's mother spent almost two years in Atlit, until she was released by the *Sochnut*, an Israeli agency. When she got out, she found Saba. They built their home in a kibbutz on the border of Gaza.

Though they left the kibbutz for moshav life for a short stint, the kibbutz ultimately called them back.

In 1944 Saba and Safta married. Two years later my mother was born.

In exchange for milk and cream, bread was delivered to the moshav weekly.

Nine years old, my mother was responsible for picking up the bread while her parents worked in the fields. She was responsible for her two younger brothers.

Each week my mother walked the kilometer to the dairy, holding a two-year-old in one arm and the hand of a six-year-old in the other, to pick up the family loaf of bread.

One day, home from the dairy, all three siblings jumped on their parents' bed, my mother's baby brother bouncing like a bean popping in the sun, until the thin mattress fell off its delicate wooden frame.

The baby fell with it. At first, silence. No breath. Then screaming.

My mother quickly put the bed together, kissed her brother's head.

When her mother returned home she found the bed askew and a purple bump on her youngest son's head.

They moved back to the kibbutz in 1950, the kibbutz movement trying to recruit people who had left during the war. Kibbutz ideology was based on socialism, everything shared – work, food, childcare – which Saba felt made for an easier life. He was a thin man, healthy enough though not particularly strong. He was happy to return to a more communal way of living.

On the moshav, you worked for yourself and your family independently.

Kibbutzim were like communes.

Moshavim like small towns.

On the moshav, kids lived at home with parents all week. On the kibbutz, kids lived in the *bet yeladim*, kid houses, during the week. Kibbutz houses were not built for large families. They were one room, a tiny kitchenette, a bathroom, a porch.

On weekends kids stayed with parents, most of their time spent on the porch. My mother's house had a metal table on the porch and a small metal roof to block the blistering sun. She ate all her meals with her family on the porch.

I ate many meals on that porch too – cucumber tomato salads, soft brown bread, cottage cheese – surrounded by Safta's *nana*, mint garden. She soaked *nana* leaves in hot water for us to drink after eating.

Every evening during dinner in the *chadar ochel*, the dining hall, my mother asked her mother, Is it Friday yet is it Friday yet?

My mother wanted to sleep at home with her family.

Sometimes Safta made cookie dough on the porch. She brought out a ceramic bowl with flour, an egg, a cup of sugar, milk, margarine. Together, she and my mother mixed the ingredients with a wooden spoon until it formed soft dough. Safta sprinkled flour on the table and on her wooden rolling pin; they rolled the dough into a fine, thin sheet.
My mother's baby brother sat in a chair at the table and watched.
My mother's other brother stuck his fingers in the bowl, pulled out chunks to eat.

They cut circles in the dough with a small drinking glass. Or Safta cut shapes, a *Magen David* or a heart, with a paring knife. They laid the cookies on a baking sheet and sprinkled a little more sugar on top.

While the cookies baked, my mother wiped the table, draped a white cloth over it for Shabbat dinner, a cloth that rested on the table for the entire next day of Shabbat.
Each Shabbat morning Safta made French toast. At the bet yeladim kids ate hard-boiled eggs and cucumber and tomato

salads. Never anything fried. They called French toast *fried bread*. When there was cocoa, Safta made hot cocoa with warm milk.

Everything special on Shabbat.

Once a month each family received toothpaste, soap, and one small package of chocolate, four squares per child.

My mother's brother inhaled his chocolate. Inhale is the word my mother uses both in Hebrew and English when talking about this kind of eating. He inhaled his chocolate, tearing off the wrapper, shoving it all into his mouth at once.

Their younger brother ate one square, wrapped up the rest to save for later. He nibbled a little bit every day like a baby mouse. He looked like a baby mouse too, thin sharp features, delicate, quiet. My mother the mama mouse.

The middle brother, the inhaler, had wider, thicker features. Features that took up space, could project sound and consume in gulps. He eyed his little brother's chocolate.

When the little brother said, You want some? he shook his head up and down.

Yes.

When I look at pictures of my mother as a child, I see her face as an adult woman, the woman I know as my mother. It looks wrong on the body of a child.

My mind knows the world was different before I existed. But my mother's face on a body I have never seen doesn't make sense to my inner timeline.

Some of my mother's friends' families also moved back to the kibbutz. The kids lived together in the bet yeladim, slept together, ate together, showered together, played together. One of the other girls had the same name as my mother. She wasn't big, but my mother, like Saba, was thin. Kids called them Fat and Skinny. My mother said the girl didn't seem to mind.

I bet she did.

When kids went to Fat's house to play, they sat on Fat's porch as she distributed candy sent from one of her relatives in the city. If someone had candy it came from the city. Candy was wealth.

Two squares of milk chocolate each, the kind with in the orange wrapper and a brown cow. Each kid got an equal amount.

Kids could be mean, but they knew the feeling of not having something someone else had.

No one was left out.

My mother's middle brother would eat his two squares fast, licking his fingers, chocolate smearing down his chin, around his cheeks. He would finish before everyone else.

Once, as he swallowed his last bite, he started crying. My mother thought he was crying for more chocolate.

Stop crying, she said.

He pointed to his chin.

Don't be such a baby, she said.

He kept crying, lifted his chin to her face. She saw a tiny stinger among the chocolate smears.

The other kids leaned in to get a look.

My mother held her brother's round face in her hands, pinched the stinger between her fingers, pulled it out. Then she gave him her second square of chocolate.

Saba worked as a truck driver in the early days of kibbutz
life. He drove to and from the city, brought cheap treats to my
mother and her brothers, *halvah* made from sesame seeds,
rahat locum gooey gelatin Turkish delight of rosewater and
pistachios.

My mother and her brothers waited for their father's truck in
late afternoons, watched for a growing dust cloud to approach
the kibbutz gate.
Aba Aba what did you bring me? The youngest brother ran to
the truck.
Shut up stupid don't yell so the world can hear, the other
brother said.
He knew kibbutz life was not abundant. It was good. It was
enough. And, there was no extra.
Old enough to know not to expect things, my mother remained
silent.

My mother used to say to me, If someone on the kibbutz
needed the shirt I was wearing, I had to give it to them. Nothing
belonged to me. I hated that.

My mother is seven years older than her youngest brother. As children, she pretended he was her baby.

I'm the ima and you are my baby, she said.

He smiled and acted like the three-year-old that he was.

My mother's other brother liked cars and tractors. He sat on the porch with lids to pots and pans, hands at ten and two, side to side like steering wheels.

My mother sat behind him on the steps. Bus driver is this the bus to Tel Aviv?

Yes you are on the right bus hold on tight here we go, he said.

He leaned back. My mother bounced her younger brother on her lap until he laughed.

My mother happily born a mother.

She wanted to be an art teacher, take care of her own kids, four of them. Four kids she wanted.

There are two of us.

I asked for a sister when I was little, but I never got one.

My mother was ten when the Suez-Sinai War between Israel

and Egypt broke, not the first conflict over this border. Not the

first, not the last, round and round no start no finish.

Tunnels built underground by soldiers for soldiers, to move

easily during combat.

My mother's family put into bomb shelters with other families,

children from the bet yeladim. They couldn't go outside for a

week.

They spent their days reading books to each other and quietly

to themselves.

At night, my mother lay in her bunk, a friend below, her

brothers across from her, and listened to the bombs explode

outside.

Maybe she closed her eyes, felt the vibrations through her

body.

Maybe she imagined her shaking metal bed a flying carpet,

each boom floating higher, wind in her hair, the smell of the

sun baking the earth.

I've heard these sounds too, from the bomb shelter at Safta's

house. This one-room bomb shelter built after I already knew

what it was for. Thick thick walls, heavy concrete, heavier air

inside. The high pitch of the bombs before the deeper booms,
I imagined were hawks and swallows, weaving geometric
patterns in the sky.
Spirals, loops, same sounds, different times, same. Like the
Fourth of July in America. Different same.

My mother wasn't scared, not yet knowing how the land would
look after the bombs. When they were little, they were taken
away during combat. They didn't have television until after the
Six-Day War, years later.

Israel won rule over Sinai.

Ownership changes depending on surrender, blood, money, power.

Same as now, same as here.

After the Suez-Sinai War, Israelis were taken on trips to
Sinai, to *Santa Catarina*, Saint Catherine's, one of the oldest
monasteries in the world. *Santa Catarina*, beige like the dusty
landscape built from stone, as if carved out of the mountains it
sat amongst.

The trip was hours long. My mother and her mother rode on
low wooden benches in the back of a truck covered with an
open-air piece of canvas, every bump from the unpaved road
felt in everyone's legs.

The truck held twelve people, six on each bench, facing each
other pulling out photo albums from the war to show.

They learned about the world from one another's stories in the
back of a truck.

Black-and-white photographs with crimped edges, looked old
even when they were new.

My mother had a friend whose uncle lived in Tel Aviv, the big city, worked in a chocolate factory. They called him Uncle Chocolate.

Uncle Chocolate came for a visit, the friend would say, with a small tub of *mimrach chocolad*, chocolate spread, in her hands. Everyone cheered.

The teacher took a loaf of day-old crusty white bread from the snack cabinet, sat the kids at a table and spread the creamy chocolate on slices. Chocolate cake.

The friend and her Uncle Chocolate, heroes.

When I was in grade school, my mother brought *mimrach chocolad* back from Israel, smeared it on thick rye bread, two pieces smooshed together and filled with chocolate, to make a sandwich. I was jealous of peanut butter and jelly, something we never had at our house. My sandwiches so delicious but I was made fun of anyway.

Until ninth grade kids ate lunch in the bet yeladim. No cafeteria in school. A teenage caretaker brought food on a little metal cart with squeaky wheels. Once in awhile there was fruit, enough for each person to have one apple or one banana. When my mother was older, orchards were planted, apples, oranges, grapefruits. After that, during harvest, boxes of fruit outside of the chadar ochel. Anyone could take some. Bigger families took more. No one took too much. Socialism still intact.

One year my mother's brother, the chocolate lover, took me to

the edge of the kibbutz, high up a hill three-sixty views covered

in citrus trees.

You can pick a grapefruit an orange a lemon, he said.

Take a deep breath, he said.

It smelled like tangy citrus aromatherapy. It smelled like peace.

He pointed to the west and said, That's Gaza.

Kitchens were the size of tiny hallways in kibbutz houses and, in the early days, no refrigerators. Most meals were eaten in the chadar ochel, everyone together at long metal tables. Soup with rice, cucumbers and tomatoes, farm cheese and bread. Sometimes chicken and noodles or matzo balls.

Aruchat arba, the four o'clock snack, the only meal at home during the week, after school. A cup of milk or tea, a sandwich with margarine and jam or a cucumber, could be taken home from the chadar ochel. After aruchat arba, kids returned to the bet yeladim to sleep for the night.

My mother was always hungry at four.

Didn't you eat lunch at the bet yeladim? her mother asked.

No it was gross.

Salty pancakes made from flour and margarine and occasionally meat, a taste that made my mother gag with a smell, she said, like dirty socks.

She hid the dirty sock pancakes in the small pockets of her dress, threw them away when no one was looking and didn't tell her mother that part.

My mother knew not to complain about food.

I was like this about food as a child too. When my mother tells me this story, I am the child and she is my safta.

Our memories one memory.

I complained about food all the time. My mother never shut me up.

Safta worked in the laundry. Back then and long as I
remember.

Women worked in the laundry when they could no longer do
manual labor. They could sit to sew, iron, fold.

The small laundry shack sat among houses along one of the
main walking paths through the kibbutz, a slight building full
of *Saftot*, grandmothers.

Families left their laundry at the end of Shabbat, Saturday, the
Sabbath, to pick back up on Friday before the next Shabbat.
One pile for dark work clothes, one for colors, one for whites,
all wrapped in a bedsheet and dropped through a window slot
on the side of the shack, a chute that ended inside in a bin
like a slide with a foam pit at the bottom. Each member had
a number and each piece of clothing, each piece of linen, was
sewn with that number.

The threadbare sheets on my bed, the ratty towels, the soft
cases so old they feel like silk holding my pillows, all have
kibbutz numbers hand sewn in their edges by my safta.
My mother still asks me if I need linens.
Yes, always yes.

They smell like the soothing sound of doves behind Safta and Saba's house on the kibbutz. And like home, my childhood home, in America.

After he drove trucks, Saba worked in the *Kol Bo*.

Kol Bo, literally *everything in it*, was a tiny general store that didn't exist until Saba worked there. He opened the store with a few others to bring more goods, more city to the country. Kibbutz members signed for what they bought, the cost deducted from their stipend.

The *Kol Bo* still existed when I was a kid. I never put together what the name meant until my mother told me this story. My American eyes unable to see *everything in it.*

Saba managed the *Kol Bo*, was the main purchaser for the kibbutz.

The *Kol Bo* did not, in fact, have everything. No clothes, no hardware supplies, no toys.

So people made requests on Fridays and Saba drove a Kibbutz car to Tel Aviv on Sundays to buy what *everything in it* did not have.

Saba never cheated anyone out of anything, my mother told me several times.

She didn't have to tell me.

I know, I said to her. I know.

Sometimes Saba took my mother and her brothers to Tel Aviv with him.

Once, he bought them ice cream and sodas along the way and after errands took them to Tnuva, a big dairy company, for lunch.

They ate sunny-side up eggs with sour cream, fluffy rolls with fresh butter, French fries and cheeses, hummus and olives.

I can't finish Aba, my mother's brother whispered. He hung his head low, worried he would be in trouble.

Just leave it, Saba said. He laughed, my mother and her brother surprised.

In the bet yeladim, not finishing food was forbidden.

Nothing wasted, no extra.

From childhood through adolescence into adulthood, Saba was skinny.

Always. In every picture. Throughout my childhood to the day he died.

We all joked about how none of us got his genes.

Because of his thinness, he was considered unhealthy. People on the kibbutz with health problems were sent to a retreat center in Haifa for a few days to relax, three meals a day, room and board, a swimming pool.

When my mother was ten, Saba gave one of his days to her so she could stay with him. My mother never had food like the food there. As a child she was thin like him, like most kibbutz children. There wasn't enough food to gain weight.

At the center they ate chicken soup.

Chicken soup was medicine, not food. On the kibbutz, meat was rare. Patties were made from bread and margarine.

After chicken soup, fluffy mashed potatoes, sugar-glazed carrots, sweet green peas, fried zucchinis, eggplant baba ghanoush, bread with real butter.

Aba, my mother said, I'm full from the soup.

With the food will come your appetite, Saba said. Smell the food. It will inspire your hunger. He waved his hand from the food to his face, smiled.

They sat next to a woman who had been my mother's caretaker at the bet yeladim when she was little.

The woman said, This food is the best. You do not leave food here. You eat a little, you rest, you eat a little more, you rest a little more. That's how it goes.

My mother thought this was a joke. But she saw the woman and other people spend hours eating and resting, eating and resting.

For dessert, vanilla ice cream or pear compote. Pears, like most fruit, were a delicacy. Sometimes they had oranges and grapefruit and apples. Never pears.

Pears were Saba's favorite. He chose compote.

No, my mother said. I want ice cream.

I will buy you ice cream another time. You don't get to choose pears every day. Pears are the most delicious, Saba said.

I don't want compote I want ice cream, my mother said.

She was ten. She didn't know that it would be a long time before she would get to eat a pear again.

My mother went to first grade in Afula on the moshav, ten kids in class and the teacher a young soldier. Teaching was one of the jobs women were given in the army.

On the first day my mother sat with her friend on one side, her friend's cousin on the other side.

That cousin was killed in the Six-Day War when they were in the army.

My mother's neighbors, also Holocaust survivors, had three kids. Two of them died in that war.

Everyone knew everyone who died in those wars. They had gone to school together or with a sister or brother or cousin. Everyone connected, woven loops.

In high school in America my best friend's father was Israeli. Thirty-something years earlier he'd been my mother's camp counselor.

Everyone still knows everyone.

Israel is the size of New Jersey.

My friend moved back to Israel in our junior year. My mother told me I cried for weeks when she left. I don't remember this. I don't remember being that attached to her.

But hearing my mother tell this story reminded me, the secret language we shared, the cultural web our parents wove long before us.

Ancestral roots tangled so deep, my memory lost them.

When my mother was in eighth grade, the kibbutz opened its own school and bussed in kids from another nearby kibbutz. School started early in the morning. Breakfast at 7 AM and lunch from the chadar ochel packed in little plastic boxes. The boxes stank from sitting closed in the heat for hours. Kids ate the food anyway. There was nothing else.

Each day before class, my mother and her friend showed one another what they had brought from home. They always shared their treats.
Sometimes the friend had rolls with chocolate cream or a chocolate bar.
Sometimes my mother had yeast cookies from Safta.
The friend's kibbutz had more money, more than my mother's silverware factory-supported kibbutz. The friend's was a German kibbutz, received reparations from Germany, from the war.

When I was a child, my mother habitually checked the backs of knives, forks, and spoons at friends' houses or at restaurants, sometimes finding her kibbutz name engraved.
Validation for the silverware factory of her past life.

In high school, kids moved out of the bet yeladim into dorms, three tiny buildings, boys on one side, girls on the other. Four kids in one room, one shared bathroom per building. The rooms were so small they smooshed all the beds against each other, like the room was one big bed. Most of their time was spent outside on the porch steps anyway, drinking Turkish coffee, spitting sunflower seed shells at each other. Or in the auditorium for dances, cafés, and after the Six-Day War, watching a black-and-white TV. Sometimes they watched American movies or TV shows.

Mostly, they held hands watching the news, hoping it wouldn't be as bad as they thought.

In 1964, the summer after she turned eighteen, my mother
was drafted for basic training in the army.

All of the kibbutz girls stuck together. *Kibbutnikim*, country
bumpkins.

They woke at 4 AM, made their beds with creased folds, perfect
on all sides.

They had group exercise, running, jumping jacks, sit-ups and
stretching.

They learned how to shoot M16s lying on their bellies aiming at
paper targets, then standing, propping the heavy rifles against
their slender shoulders.

When I was sixteen I went to a camp led by the Israeli army. I
also shot M16s at paper targets. The heaviness of the gun in
my arms made me feel strong.

I couldn't imagine shooting a person or an animal, but I
understood how someone could feel powerful, in control behind
a gun.

My friends and I compared our targets, spread them side
by side, touching the bullet holes in the thin paper with our
fingers.

Year after year my family asked me if I would return when I was eighteen to join the army.

Maybe, I always said.

I knew I never would.

My mother kept her olive green uniform ironed and creased
more than she was required to, stiff and crisp. It felt important.
They hiked in the morning before the sun came up, carried
each other's jerry cans when they got too tired, cleaned outdoor
latrines, rarely complaining. Their parents' struggles from
World War II were still close.

They were happy to be old enough to support the only place
their families could go to escape death.

After two months of basic training, my mother and her friends were sent to a dorm in Jerusalem to learn to be teachers. They still wore crisp green uniforms and carried M16s, but the physical struggles of army life were over. They went to classes in a building with tile floors and indoor plumbing, days filled with books and studying at desks.

In December, my mother and her classmates lit a menorah, gambled at dreidel with peanuts, and sang Hanukkah songs over potato latkes with apple sauce.

My mother learned how to be an elementary school teacher in the army. She was sent to Ofakim in the Negev, not far from the kibbutz, where she got an apartment with three other *kibbutznik* teachers.

Each morning my mother put on her freshly ironed army uniform and walked or hitchhiked to the school to teach second grade. No one had a car or money for the bus.

The kids reminded my mother of when she was little with her brothers.

I really loved teaching, my mother told me.

When she talks about this time, her eyes sparkle.

I believe her nostalgia. And, I know memory has a mind of its own.

Magical times interweave seamlessly with the challenges we want to forget.

On the weekends, my mother hitchhiked home to the kibbutz to stay with her parents. Safta sent her back each week with fresh baked margarine cookies or a cream cake to share with her roommates.

The army provided a small stipend for bills and groceries. My mother and her roommates shopped at the market down the street from their apartment. They guys at the market wrote down what they bought and at the end of the month, when they received their stipend, they paid up in cash. Usually the bill was more money than they thought it would be. At one point they realized they were getting ripped off.
They never said anything.

After they paid all the bills, the rent, and the guys at the market, they pooled together the few shekels they had left and split them evenly.
Communal, like the kibbutz.
They cleaned the apartment together, made soup together, went to parties together. The same way they grew up.

The Six-Day War happened in 1967 around Egypt, Jordan, Syria. My mother's brother was sent to fight in Sinai near the Suez Canal.

My mother was just out of the army, living in the kibbutz in a studio apartment, a room with a bathroom and a porch.

Everyone was scared for my uncle. At that time the only TV was the little black-and-white one in the auditorium. News was sparse, information was word of mouth.

They worried. And also, they weren't overwhelmed with information.

A lot of waiting, asking around, listening to each other's stories to get news.

I remember this from my childhood too.

In 1980s America we watched infinite TV, talked endlessly on the phone.

In Israel phone numbers were four digits long and only a few hours of TV a day. The phone was to be used quickly, and if you turned on the TV during a lull, there was a rainbow circle with a high-pitched beep on all three channels.

When my mother returned to the kibbutz after the army, she started dating a guy from the next kibbutz over.

He is mostly detail-less. Except that his parents took him and my mother to Tel Aviv to see *Doctor Zhivago* in English, with subtitles. I might be making this up. This movie always seems to be the one people of my parents' generation talk about seeing on dates. I've never seen it.

They went on double dates with the guy's brother and his brother's girlfriend and visited each other's kibbutzim.

He was handsome I liked him and there were lots of others just like him, my mother said.

My mother was a beauty and she knew it.
Her clock did not need to tick.

As a child, I remember thinking my mother was so much more beautiful than my friends' mothers, which she was.

My father was sent to the kibbutz during the Six-Day War to work on combines harvesting wheat. He was thirty to my mother's twenty-three, long done with the army. During wartime, you could volunteer to help wherever it was needed. War was imminent, always, which made the army a constant in so much of what people did.

When I was little, my mother's brother was assigned to security for the kibbutz. He had a key to the ammunition shed. My mother called it the ammunition closet. I imagine an entire collection of machine guns and bullets stored in a small, rusty tin shed with a padlock.

Part of my uncle's job was *shmirat liyla*, night watch. He was in charge of general security and of the soldiers that came to the kibbutz over the years, but *shmirat liyla* was a job most of the men on the kibbutz were also required to do every six months or so for the duration of a week. During *shmirat liyla*, two guys worked together. One guy had a gun and sat in a tiny booth, like a tollbooth with a glass window, late into the night. He guarded the one entrance to the one dirt road that made a loop around the kibbutz. The rest of the kibbutz was enclosed by a chain-link fence. The other guy patrolled the outskirts.

The kibbutz was on the border of Gaza, conflicting sides close.

Once, bombers got into the kibbutz and stole water pipes from the farm fields, but no one was hurt.

Killings and kidnappings were not rare on other kibbutzim.

I've wondered if my uncle ever had to use the gun. Or if anyone ever pointed a gun at him. I never asked, too scared to know.

My father worked with a guy who knew my mother.

You have to introduce me to her, he said.

Only if you stay to live on the kibbutz, the guy said.

I promise I will I just have to meet that girl, my father said.

The night my parents were introduced, a landmine killed a guy from my mother's class. People died all the time. You get used to death, but the way it feels doesn't change. If you didn't know the person who died, you knew someone close.

The brother of the guy who stepped on the landmine had died in the war the month before.

Someone was always dying.

Grieving began again, overlapping the previous death.

Romance seemed redundant next to the weight of the war. But
my mother liked my father's black-rimmed, coke-bottle glasses.
She liked his excitement about combines and the grease his
work left in the cracks of his hands.
She liked the way nothing was too much for him when
everything was too much for everyone else, and how he looked
at her like he would always be around.
She liked his stupid jokes.

My father took my mother to the beach on a motorcycle he
fixed up.
He took my mother on that motorcycle to Tel Aviv for falafel,
to Haifa to the Baha'i Temple circular garden, to float on the
surface of the salty Dead Sea, and then to Jerusalem to meet
his parents.

I have never seen my mother on a motorcycle in real life.
There are three pictures of my parents on a motorcycle trip and
she doesn't look scared in any of them. In my life my mother
fears, maybe hates, motorcycles. Maybe having children
stimulated her distaste.
As a child I sat on the gas tank of my father's old Yamaha,
padded by my diaper and a huge old helmet, ready for a ride

around the block anytime. He took all the neighborhood kids for rides.

The only time my mother had been to Jerusalem was for her training in the army. She was a *kibbutznik,* a country girl. Jerusalem, the serious city, big like Tel Aviv but heavy, religious, hard.

Jerusalem reminds me of my father's mother.

My father's parents came from Russia before World War II.

My father's father sold oranges. And in the early days, he was a street sweeper.

My father's mother was a serious pianist. She was tall with a puffed chest and did not smile at my mother when they met. She wore her hair in a stern bun at the back of her head and she looked at my mother as though she was not good enough for her son.

This is also how I remember my grandmother. I vaguely remember her smile.

But my father loved my mother in a way that didn't concern his parents.

Besides all of it, my mother's name is the same as my father's, with an *a*, or a letter *hey* in Hebrew, on the end.

When my father finished his volunteer service on the kibbutz
he had to go back to work in Tel Aviv. His motorcycle had
broken down and my mother didn't have a car.
Neither had the money to go back and forth by bus.
Hitchhiking was too much waiting, and people hitchhiking
started to disappear.
The conflict rose, everyone fighting for a place in the middle of
the middle of the desert.
My parents drifted apart.

But my mother did not forget about my father. My father did not forget about my mother.

She dated other people. He dated other people.

Neither of them forgot.

Six months after their split, my mother sent my father a postcard. She would be in Tel Aviv for a class. Would he meet her?

My father pulled up to my mother's class on a different motorcycle.

My mother got on behind him and stayed.

My mother was happy to be on the kibbutz, close to her parents. Home.

She wasn't in a hurry to marry, but working with kids reminded her of the family she longed to have.

And then, my father got his papers for America.

He talked about it. It was 1969. He didn't say he wanted space from his family. He didn't say he was sick of the wars. He didn't say anything about what he would leave behind or why he wanted to leave it. Only what was ahead.

Opportunity. Education and money.

America.

In Israel, everyone had to learn English.

My mother was dyslexic. Her own language, her life in Israel, wars and all, were enough. English only confused things.

She had not forgotten her parents' struggles to make a good life.

A new country with a new language and a new culture far from family were not on her list of life goals.

No, she said when my father asked her to go to America.

Please, he said.

One week after my father moved to the U.S. his letters started arriving.

After the first one, they came every day.

Each day Safta collected the family mail and each day she went to the *gan yeladim* where my mother worked with a letter from America.

My father wrote about the snow in Chicago. He wrote about the tiny apartment in an enormous city you couldn't imagine, about skyscrapers, greasy burgers, so many flavors of ice cream. He wrote about how he missed my mother. How he loved her.

Again, he asked her to come to America.

My mother knew she wouldn't stay.

It would only be a visit.

One time and that would be the end of their affair.

My father bought my mother a ticket to America. When she arrived, he cancelled the return flight and said, You're staying. My mother wasn't sure. But she knew she loved him.

2.

During the week my cousins stayed in a separate house with a big shower room and five sets of bunk beds to a room. Same as it was when my mother was a child. Nobody, including the teenage caretaker, wore shoes.

Outside, the ground was dusty, a reminder there weren't always plants and buildings there. Not until after our grandparents.

Inside, all the doorknobs long and skinny like in Europe, not like in America where they're round to fit your palm. This always felt superior to me, a long doorknob. I don't know why.

Each bet yeladim was named after a fruit: *Duvdevan*, cherry. *Toot sadeh*, strawberry. The floors were speckled tile, the buildings gritty plaster.

We ate cucumbers and cheese at little wooden tables and, on lucky days, a few squares of milk chocolate, the kind with the cow on the orange wrapper.

I didn't have to stay there but I liked to, to be with my cousins and my summer friends. My grandparents' house was small, two rooms.

I wanted to be barefoot, to wear my long hair wild, the reason I had head lice at the end of the summer. Every. Single. Year.

I spent all of my childhood summers there.

In the fall, waiting in line at school in America, scratching my head, finding bugs under my nails, praying the nurses' thick glasses and plastic gloves wouldn't find them.

They always did.

I sat on the toilet next to the window in our house, my mom running her fingers through my dirty hair, pulling out bugs and crushing them between her nails. The sound, a little click for each bug and her cursing in Hebrew, threatening to cut off all my hair, which finally happened one year. An end to toxic chemicals in the shower, but I cried for my hair.

Sometimes the Midwest smells like the Middle East in the heat of summer.

The smell of, nothing matters but this moment.

You might not think of the Middle East like that if you only know it from the news.

Experience has more dimensions than media. You don't know the whole thing unless you can feel it on your skin, through the holes in your face.

I can feel it.

I waited all year to go to the other side of the world. Every summer on the last day of school I couldn't believe the time had arrived.

Childhood time so slow, summer lasts forever, winter is epic.

Maybe we are more present in childhood.

My mom packed three enormous suitcases, the ones with buckles and without wheels. One with her and my dad's clothes, one with mine and my brother's, one with gifts from America.

In the eighties you couldn't get Nikes and Levis in Israel.

My mom woke us in the middle of the night to go to the airport.

My dad lugged the suitcases to the front door to wait for the cab.

My mom hauled our bags of toys and snacks, gum, hard candies, chocolate.

We flew on EL AL, the Israeli airline. They opened all the suitcases, undoing my mom's hours of Tetris puzzling to make everything fit.

Always made-for-TV movies about airplane terrorists back then.

My brother and I slept on the thin carpeted floor at the gate, near the windows. We got emergency exit row seats so we could continue to sleep the twelve hour ride on the thin carpeted floor of the plane.

In that era, when you could walk someone all the way to the gate, before the security of no shampoo, no shoes, no belts, no water, 9/11, my grandparents waited at the Ben Gurion International Airport gate.

When planes were hijacked and still, there was more trust.

Sometimes my uncle was there too, with a bag of candy. My mom pointed them out in the clutter of people. I ran toward them like I hadn't seen them in a decade. How a year is a lifetime.

Safta pinched my cheeks, Saba smelled like he smells, like a sweet old man who works in a silverware factory and loves me. His face scraggly with beard shadow sanding my sensitive baby skin but I liked it. I liked being small and light and squeezed.

We piled our suitcases and ourselves into a skinny Peugeot
van borrowed for the day from the kibbutz, warm air gliding in
through the car windows, the smell of sage baking in the sun.
I looked up at the palm tree fronds, green against aqua sky,
familiar, home. My body tingled.
In Israel, like in some of Europe, street curbs are painted in
stripes, the roads and cars smaller, narrower.
Everything, everyone, takes up less space.

Outside and inside blended, open-air flea markets and patios.
First thing after jetlag, falafel in Sderot, twenty bottomless
salads, ferments, sesame sauces and pickles you stuff into
a giant pita filled with the fried garbanzo balls and chips,
pronounced *cheeps*, French fries.

On the way to the kibbutz we stopped at my great-aunt's house
in Lod, her crooked teeth just like Safta's teeth, and a face that
always seemed to be in a close-up. The smell of her cinnamon
cookies everywhere, inside and outside blended, plants all over
the massive white concrete porch connecting her house to her
son's family's house.

My second cousins lived there, the grandchildren of Safta's sister. They were older than me. Their skin was two shades darker brown than mine, even without the sun, and they were always taller and thinner than me. I wanted to look like them, to look like I belonged there, for my body to represent the culture of my ancestors.

My second cousins had a little dog, Bobee. Bobee shit in the house. The first time I stepped in shit barefoot, maybe the only time, I was ten. An age where this could make me cry or be hilarious, depending on the witness.

The witness was my mom and she laughed hard. I love when my mom laughs. She loses her breath, holds her chest and says my name like she can't believe what I've said or done. She washed my feet in the tub, laughing, then we sat on the porch swing eating my great-aunt's cinnamon cookies, laughing, laughing.

The first night at Saba and Safta's house on the kibbutz, always sleepless. I lay in the makeshift couch bed, Safta's and my father's snores vibrated through the floor, the couch, around my body, in my skull. Occasionally mom's snores. The whole tiny house shook, a tonal chorus of heavy breathing. In the morning I told them all they snored. Everyone denied it and laughed. I knew they knew. Everyone except Saba. He was still a skinny, quiet man.

First thing on the first day the swimming pool, a quick walk up the path behind my grandparents' house, just around the dark pink Bougainvillea.

When the kibbutz kids arrived, we hugged and they asked me about America, sometimes calling it *Anglia*, England, thinking about speaking English. Always wide-eyed when I told them about having my own room and all the TV channels.

This happened every year until we hit puberty.

Puberty ruined everything.

Even when I had to wear hand-me-downs, even when I didn't get toys I wanted, I knew how privileged I was. I knew how hard my parents worked, what they left behind.

I also envied my kibbutz friends, the kibbutz full of blooming flower meadows and grandparents and running wild.

Someone would count, *shalosh, arba, ve...* (three, four, and...) and we all jumped in. We swam the length of the pool underwater holding our breath. Who could go the farthest, who could hold a handstand the longest, who could do a backflip? We all did them all.

When we got tired we went to the pool kiosk for *artik* and *cartives*, popsicles and ice creams. I signed them out on Saba's name, conscious not to take too many, knowing Saba and Safta would have to pay for them with their small kibbutz stipend.

Once, I did a swan dive into the pool from the side, not quite the deep end, to show off. My chin hit the bottom, a smack and my skull rattled, blood oozed from my bottom lip where my teeth had bitten down.

The wetness of blood with the wetness of water.

I ran down the path to Saba and Safta's house, hot tears down my face. As I ran through the pool gates I heard kids yelling behind me, What happened what happened she hit her chin in the pool I saw blood!

One year, someone spotted a turd in the water and all the kids yelled, *Kaki kaki*! Poop poop! We evacuated the pool and everyone started blaming everyone. The culprit was never discovered.

After the pool, my brother and I fought over who got to shower first.

In the tiny bathroom, the toilet flushed by turning a knob, watching a rush of water fill the bowl, then turning the knob off when it seemed enough had come in. I liked how trusted I was to manually guide my *kaki* into the sewer.

The toilet was next to the shower, which was next to the sink, no barrier around the shower to keep the water contained, just a drain in the middle of the bathroom floor. After every shower, my mom squeegeed the whole wet floor toward the drain.

Every year I asked my mom why they didn't build a barrier around the shower. She always said, I don't know that's just how they built it.

We ate dinner in the chadar ochel. Upstairs was the kitchen and eating area, giant windows at two ends of the open room with long metal tables arranged in rows, everyone eating family style, kibbutz style. When you finished eating, you scraped any remnants into a big trash can and put the dirty dishes on a conveyer belt that went back into the kitchen to be washed. Downstairs, personal mailboxes and bulletin boards with flyers for movies showing on a small screen at the café. The café, in the back of the building on the first floor, was where teenagers hung out, kids home from the army and those about to get drafted.

They drank coffee and beer and smoked cigarettes and gossiped.

They were cool, I wanted to belong, but knew I never would.

I would never go to the army and not going to the army excluded you from everything.

The army made a person Israeli, transitioned a teenager into an adult.

TV happened once a day, a kid's show in the early evening, then the news, then an American movie at night. If you had a TV in your house. Saba and Safta had one. My cousins had one too. Sometimes we went to watch at their house on the other side of the kibbutz. An American movie was big, all the kids sitting together to watch even though my brother and I had probably seen it the year before, Back to the Future or Cocoon.

Israel was still in the seventies during the eighties, still in the eighties during the nineties.

No one was allowed to talk or sit in Saba's chair, a thin swiveller with plaid upholstery and brown leather trim, when the news came on.

The news made Saba a different man.

The news made him yell at us to shut up if we made noise.

Even during commercials.

That famous commercial – *altigah chefetz chashud!* – don't pick up a foreign object on the street! It could be a bomb.

And then, on the news, some kid blown up by a random bag on the street.

At three o'clock each afternoon, thick shutters and windows were shut tight and adults went to sleep.

We rode our bikes in the scorching desert heat through the kibbutz pathways and around the main road, hot air blowing our hair into tangles, browning our skin, freckling our faces. We rode away from the houses, away from the adults, quiet in the wind.

We rode around the edges, around sunflower fields, the animal sanctuary with free roaming peacocks and to the pea garden where we stuffed raw peas into our mouths. We visited the citrus grove at the top of the hill, eating oranges and grapefruits straight off the tree while looking over the border to Gaza.

Quiet in the wind, no bomb sounds, no smoke. Not then not yet.

Twenty years later, bomb shelters and ruin and all the people I once knew moved away or dead.

3.

My father grew up in Jerusalem. Opposite of kibbutz life.
Jerusalem the bigger big city, bigger than Tel Aviv, heavy with
religious smog, gray even in a cloudless sky.
My father grew up in the back apartment of a concrete,
L-shaped building with his mother, father and brother.
His grandparents lived in the two-story apartment at the front
of the building. His saba had a clinic in the upstairs of the
apartment and they lived downstairs.
My father told me about a brass microscope his saba let him
look through, my father in his little boy coke-bottle glasses.
There is a picture of him with those thick, round specs, clear
rings around his eyes that remind me of crazy straws from my
own childhood.

My father's aunt lived in the apartment above my father.
My father's aunt, my grandmother's sister, the only one in his
family who could cook like the women in my mother's family.

There was one more apartment on the third floor, above the
clinic. My father remembers an old lady. Her apartment had a
door to the rooftop balcony where the water tanks sat.
The old woman lived alone with a shiny Siamese cat who fell
from the balcony and didn't land on his feet. The cat survived

but walked crooked after that, and had a funny eye.

I still thought the cat was beautiful, my father told me.

Jerusalem was a two-hour drive from the kibbutz, skirting around the West Bank, windy roads up dry mountain passes. My father borrowed a tiny Peugeot from the kibbutz to drive us through the narrow city streets to his childhood home. The same as it was when he was a boy, minus his father, plus a black rotary phone, and my safta there alone, longer than I was ever alive.

My father's father was born in 1900, a communist in the
Russian Revolution of 1920, left as Stalin arrived, his place no
longer what he knew it to be. He escaped to Israel/Palestine,
never went back to Russia, never talked about it.
He died of pancreatic cancer one month before my parents
were married. They had to change their wedding date.

A famous picture of him in black and white, wild hair, cigarette
hanging out of his mouth, holding my father wrapped in a
blanket.
Maybe there was no cigarette, but usually there was.
Famous pictures relative to photo albums and my memories
remind me of stories my mother told me.
I never knew that saba, never called him *Saba*, but I knew he
smoked, he was funny, and he was always in black and white.

When my father's mother was put into hospice, my father

packed her home, his childhood, her life — books, papers,

documents, in Hebrew, English, German, Russian, Yiddish, a

lifetime of alphabets and numbers and pages.

He found his father's papers, papers he had never seen, buried

deep inside old wooden desk drawers.

My father's father was born in 1898. Not 1900.

Why did he lie? I asked my father.

I don't know, he sighed. I don't know.

I like to think he was a friend of Emma Goldman, blacklisted

during the Russian Revolution, that his Jewish, Russian,

political, immigrant status connected him to the pieces of

history that inspire me, the people I came from who made

progress through struggle the way my parents struggled.

I like to think he liked to think like me.

My Jerusalem safta was much younger than her husband. Whenever my father asked his mother about his father, she said, I was too young to remember and he never told me. Which may have been true. Or not. She wasn't one to tell stories.

My father never met his paternal grandparents. They stayed in Russia. He asked about them when he was five, ten, fifteen, twenty. His father didn't want to talk about them, never told my father their names.

As the generations grow, the stories shrink smaller and smaller, until the story is just one sentence long: I don't know.

When I asked my father about his childhood, he talked about his twenties. I asked again, he told me one small thing, then back to his twenties.

He doesn't remember his childhood, my mother said.

Or he doesn't want to tell me.

Or he doesn't want to remember.

My father's mother, my other safta, was a classical pianist,
strict stern disciplined, her hair always in place, both as an old
lady and in pictures of her youth.

Hers was science music, conventional, creative but not artsy,
not religious.

Jerusalem, engulfed in a haze of prayer woven around threads
of atheism.

Religion is the cause of all war, my father said. Many times.

Safta's black piano had a round stool painted black to match, spun right or left to move up or down. I spun until someone told me to stop and play the piano instead.

The piano against the wall of the library, filled floor to ceiling with books in all the languages she spoke, read, wrote, so many books I wish I could go back and pay attention.

I wish I could go back, listen to her strong voice read to me in languages I don't understand. I wish I could go back, watch her speckled hands unpeel ancient yellowed pages. I wish I could go back and remember.

My father and his brother slept in the sitting room, a sofa by day, a bed by night.

Next to the sitting room, Safta slept in a closed porch filled with plants and mosquitos. (Mosquitos still there by the time I was around, buzzed inside my ears, maybe inside hers. I never slept through the night in that house.) My father's father slept in the one bedroom of the apartment.

By the time I was there, it was Safta's room, and it had a door with a milk glass window, like it belonged in a doctor's office. Her narrow, fluffy bed covered in a bright red blanket, year after year, the same blanket.

I don't remember my parents ever sleeping in the same room, my father told me.

There was a short hallway with crooked ceramic tiles that eventually became loose and clanked when stepped on. The dark hallway extended from the front of the apartment to the bathroom, ending at the kitchen, a small room with a round table squeezed between the icebox and the doorway to the hall. The toilet in a small room on its own, the sink and tub next to it in another room. Like in Europe.

This made no sense to me as a child. The toilet room was claustrophobic with a long pull handle and a high-up window that seemed unreachable by anyone. A tall, rectangular box. It makes more sense to me now, you can shit while someone's in the shower.

My father's mother made plain omelets, scrambled eggs with white cheese, chicken soup, *shniztel, palachinkas* — crepes filled with cheese.
They didn't have a lot of vegetables in the city. Beige and yellow the primary colors of their diet.

My father liked plain *palachinkas*, asked his mother to leave a few empty for him.
He said, At one point my father started to eat noodles and cheese every day for some reason and I hated this food. To this day I can't stand noodles and cheese.

I have never seen my father eat anything resembling macaroni and cheese. And my mother never made this dish for me as a child.
Even though I grew up in America, there are some things I missed, some children's books in English and certain processed foods, like boxed macaroni and cheese.

You don't eat when you're hungry you eat when it's time to eat,
Jerusalem Safta told me.

She cut yellow grapefruits in half sprinkled with white sugar
and a sharp-toothed spoon.

I was fond of those pointy spoons but hated the sugar on top.

She made scrambled eggs with soft white cheese I didn't want
to eat. And some other beige foods.

Or she took us out to eat, Chinese food in the city we could
walk to from her house.

Jerusalem Safta was a woman about town.

Everywhere we went people knew Safta, my mother said.

She was a big deal, she started a music academy, won awards,
spoke at conferences. Pictures of Safta with politicians,
important people shaking hands and standing up in front
of crowds holding plaques. Crisp, yellowed photos spanning
decades, but her hair always the same, perfectly in place.

Jerusalem Safta, hard like Jerusalem, was also cats and flowers, strays that cried at her back door, the brisk *shhtk* sounds she made to scare them away.
Don't touch them they're dirty, she said to me, the person who always picked them up and tickled their heads.
And then she put out a bowl of milk out for them on the back porch.

The same back porch Safta took me out to as the sun went down, to see *Malkat Ha'liyla,* Queen of the Night blooming in the dark, just once a year. *Malkat Ha'liyla* shaped like a passionflower with delicate layers and tiny white hairs, vanilla and jasmine, allowed only whispers, no loud talking.
I thought this mattered, that the flower wouldn't bloom if we talked too loud.

Safta died two weeks shy of her ninety-eighth birthday in the midst of dementia.
I never asked her about her life.
She was always too far away, even when I was with her.
I wish I could go back to this too.

I inherited the red blanket that covered her bed through the years of my childhood. And I remember a heavy bronze ashtray in the shape of a fly, each of its wings dusty with cigarette ash. When she went into hospice, all I wanted was that fly ashtray. But no one knew where it was.

4.

When my father arrived in America in 1968, he lived in a one-bedroom apartment with another Israeli who was waiting for his wife to immigrate. My father slept on the couch.

My mother came the following summer, the summer of '69. I think of this as the year my parents came to America, and also the Vietnam War resistance, free love hippie flower power, the Age of Aquarius, Woodstock, Janis Joplin.
For my parents, it was just the year they came to America.

My father found a basement apartment on the north side of Chicago through a woman named Mrs. Julia. Mrs. Julia told my father they could not live together in the apartment unless they were married.

My father told Mrs. Julia they were engaged. They weren't.

My mother wasn't even sure she would stay.

My mother wanted to go to college but her kibbutz high school diploma was not recognized as a valid in America. And it was in Hebrew. No one could read it. My father heard about a guy who could translate documents. The guy didn't know Hebrew. He told my father to translate it himself and he would stamp it as legitimate.

Everything was paper and stamps and handshakes in the sixties.

My mother went to college. So my father went to college too. He drove a cab around Chicago part-time, worked at a picture frame manufacturer part-time, and got his master's degree in night school part-time.

My mother took art history classes and taught Hebrew to kids in the suburbs.

She met other Israelis in college and through teaching jobs, collected a Hebrew-speaking immigrant community, people I have known all my life, people we celebrate Passover and Rosh Hashanah with every year.

New family to fill the space of those missed across the ocean. I have never shared these holidays with my grandparents.

When my brother was born, three years before me, my mother began to realize Israel would not likely be her home again. By the time I was born, she knew this to be true. Knew my father's empty promises of we'll go back next year next year next year, would never come.

She considered taking us and going back without him, knowing he would follow, knowing how hard it would be, how resentful my father might become.

Every winter of my childhood in Chicago my mother said:

I hate this fucking snow.

Christmas is so materialistic.

I don't understand these American names.

Whenever I had trouble in school, my mother criticized the American school system. Whenever I pretended to be sick so I could stay home with her, my mother called in and said to me, Sometimes we just need a day off.

My mother's father fell ill the year my mother turned sixty. My father and I were planning a surprise party for her, something we had never done. Just before her birthday, my mother went to Israel to be with her father. Her father died within the month.

I did not surprise my mother.

I did not see my grandfather. I hadn't seen him in ten years.

I thought about living in Israel when I was nineteen. My mother said she would follow me if I went. She had friends who had gone back. Their kids followed them.

When I reminded her of this conversation, she said, That's not true I never said that.

Our memories woven together, mine fills in for her, hers for mine.

It was the mid-nineties, suicide bombings growing exponentially, buses exploding, cafés getting blasted, Hamas rising.

I didn't go.

There is a hole in my body, under my ribcage, around my organs.

Sometimes I dream in Hebrew. When I wake, the hole is temporarily filled.

I rise, I read the newspaper, listen to the radio, walk down the street, talk to people in English, tears in the thin hole wall begin again.

There is no one way.

No one straight line, no one yes no, no one is isn't.

Delicate sheets shield the timeline of our stories, protect our hearts, make our distance, our loops, our spirals bearable.

Same different same.

We are not made of angles. We are made of woven memory circles.

Acknowledgments:

This book would not exist without my parents, Drora and Dror, who kindly gave me their stories to make art with, and who worked so hard my entire life. Thank you Ima ve Aba.

To my amazing friends, thank you:

Sts for years of weekly writing over spiked coffee and vegan treats. You've always inspired me. I miss you.

Julie Strand for always unknowingly saying the right thing to keep me writing.

Miriam McNamara for endless coffee, gossip, and deep writing process talks.

Emily Saltzman and Rose Farrar for keeping the jew talks alive.

Joanne and Jim at Royal Grounds for creating the warmest coffee shop "office" in town, where so much of this book was written.

Thank you Molly Fuller for quick and tight editing skills.

Thank you Christina Kubasta for choosing my work, Kylie Jorgensen for being a great liaison communicator, and everyone at the Muriel Press.

And of course, Abby Beasley, my partner, my bestie, my favorite flavor, thank you for believing in me, for making so much space for me, and for buying me flowers and all the Prosecco. You are my glue when my sticky is tired and dried up. Thank you and I love you forever.

Made in the USA
Las Vegas, NV
12 January 2023

65442606R00080